Making Pedals

Making Guitar Pedals: Your First Pedal

Gerhard Weiß

Making Guitar Pedals: Your First Pedal

Copyright © Gerhard Weiß

Making Guitar Pedals: Your First Pedal
Gerhard Weiß

© 2012, Gerhard Weiß & Gary Joel White
www.sites.google.com/site/makingguitarpedals
gary909@gmail.com

ALL RIGHTS RESERVED. This book contains material protected under International and Federal Copyright Laws and Treaties. Any unauthorized reprint or use of this material is prohibited. No part of this book may be reproduced or transmitted in any form or by any means, electronic or mechanical, including photocopying, recording, or by any information storage and retrieval system without express written permission from the author / publisher.

Every precaution has been made while writing this book, the publisher and the author can assume no responsibility for errors or omissions, or for damages resulting from the information contained within.

About This Guide

If you'd like to learn how to make a guitar pedal but have no idea how then you've picked up the right guide! This book is a great way to get started in discovering a fun and highly rewarding pastime, even if you've no experience in electronics at all.

We'll take you through all the steps of building your first guitar pedal without any complicated circuit diagrams that put so many first timers off.

Contents

1. Your First Pedal
2. What We'll Need
3. Making the Case
4. Making the Circuit
5. Attaching the Circuit to the Case
6. F.A.Q

Your First Pedal

The pedal we're going to build is probably the simplest of all guitar pedals, but don't let that put you off: To make a more complicated pedal is only a minor step up. Once you've completed this book you'll already have gained a large part of the needed experience in case-building, soldering, and circuit building, plus a deeper knowledge and understanding of how it all comes together. Now lets stop wasting time & get started! Oh yeah by the way, the pedal we're building is a killswitch/stutter pedal.

What We'll Need

Lets Go Shopping!

First things first we're obviously going to need some tools to make a pedal: "But what?" I hear you asking. Nothing to exotic, don't worry! I imagine you may even have the majority of these;

Tools List

Drill
Preferably electric, but a hand powered drill is also ok.

Drill Bits:
We'll be using size 2, 5, 6, & 8.

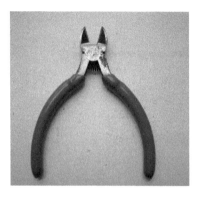

Wire Cutters:
To cut wire!

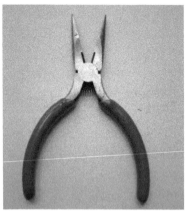

Long Nose Pliers:
For holding & bending the wire.

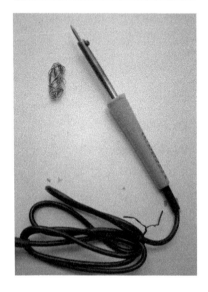

Soldering Iron with a Stand & Solder:
The cheapest soldering irons can be a right pain to use, I'd recommend at least one up from the cheapest model.

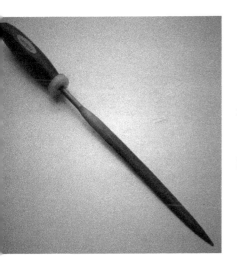

Small Rounded File:
For Filing down our pedal enclosure.

Small Screwdriver:
For the screws on the bottom of the case.

Helping Hands:
Although not essential, helping hands make this project like a million times easier. If not you can tape down objects to a desk.

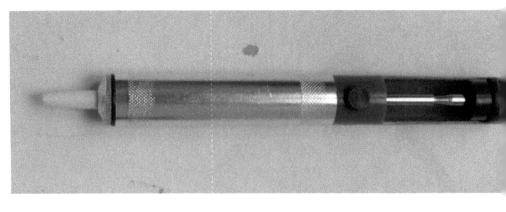

Solder Sucker:

This will help us suck up any bad solder. Alternatively you could you use solder-flux.

Other things:

You might also need a pen, ruler, box-cutters & some paper masking tape.

Parts List For The Pedal

Now we have the tools we just need the parts to make the pedal. I've listed part numbers for the UK (www.maplin.co.uk), Europe (www.banzaimusic.com) & Radio Shack for the USA (www.radioshack.com), or you can help me out **massively** & buy the parts directly from me, got to;

www.sites.google.com/site/makingguitarpedals/

You can obviously get these parts from other suppliers, or for part hunting Ebay can be pretty great. Just make sure you order the correct parts, otherwise it can be a nightmare trying to figure out why something isn't working.

Pedal Parts List

x2 Quarter-Inch (1/4") Mono Jack Input Sockets
So we can plug in the guitar!

Maplin Part No:	**HF91Y**
Banzai Music Part No:	**17593**
Radio Shack Part No:	**274-255**

x1 Push to Break Switch

This foot-switch will be providing the 'magic' to our pedal (by cutting the signal when stepped upon).

Maplin Part No:	**FH60Q**
Banzai Music Part No:	**24211**
Radio Shack Part No:	**275-1566**

20cm (roughly) of 22 Gauge Solid Copper Wire

The wire will link the components together in blissful harmony (we hope). I'm using black & red but you can use whatever you think looks cool.

Maplin Part No:	**BL85G** (blk) **BL92A** (red)
Banzai Music Part No:	25516 (blk) 25515 (red)
Radio Shack Part No:	278-1221

Some sort of Case

I'm using a Plastic Project Box that's 79 x 62 x 39mm. This case is slightly to small for the jacks to fit directly opposite each other, but I like how compact it is, so I'll be working around this limitation.

Maplin Part No:	**LH20W**
Banzai Music Part No:	23452 (121x56x31mm)
Radio Shack Part No:	270-1801

x4 Stick-on Feet

There's nothing more annoying than a pedal that slides away from you (except one that doesn't work). These feet will stop the pedal from moving.

Maplin Part No:	**FE32**
Banzai Music Part No:	**17502**
Radio Shack Part No:	**64-2346**

Making The Case

Make Your Case Heard.

For your first pedal I'd recommend using a plastic enclosure as it's loads easier to drill. If you're feeling daring you could try metal or even some old sweet tin etc, whatever floats your boat.

To start we need to decide where to put the push switch. I'd say go for the standard pedal placement: the lower middle. The centre could also be used but bear in mind that this is the weakest point of the enclosure. So, lets get to work on this bad boy:

1. I like to roughly lay down some paper masking tape as it helps prevent scratches & it's easy to

draw over. So let's do that now: mark out a strip for the foot switch and then for the two input jacks.

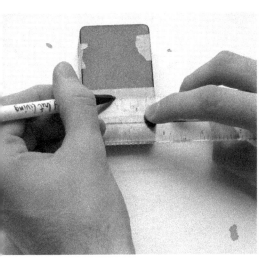

2. Use a ruler to measure where the centre of the pedal is. The pedal in the photo is about 5cm across so I've halved that and marked a line at 2.5cm. Next I've added a vertical line for more drilling precision.

3. Now do the same for the input jacks. You may notice from the picture that one of my input jack markings is lower than the other, that's because this is a small case & I don't want the jacks touching one another. If they do touch then our foot switch will not cut the signal (although we'll have made a pedal that can extend the length of guitar leads).

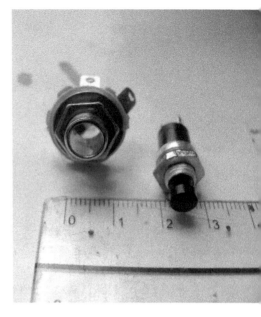

4. Before we start drilling we need to know how big to make the holes. Use the ruler to see the width of the parts that will be sticking out from the pedal. The switch should be about 6mm & the jacks about 8mm. So that means the drill bits we need are marked '6' & '8' (if they're not marked you can measure the width with the ruler). You may have noticed the width of the switch & jacks are slightly more than 6 & 8mm, but I like to file the excess down for the tightest fit - we don't want wobbly jacks or for the footswitch to fall through.

Using The Drill

Now the fun begins - It's time to drill this bad boy. But first **a word of warning**: Its also the most dangerous part of the project, so please be really very *very* careful when operating the drill. I don't want to hear any stories of drills going through hands or anything horrible like that. Got that? If you've never used a drill before go test on an old bit of wood to get a feel for it. If you have any doubts about your abilities then go find someone that can give you a lesson before starting this project.

You should also drill onto a surface that you don't mind ruining, if you don't have a suitable desk try an old wood block or even a book that you don't need.

5. The drill sizes 6 & 8mm are too big to get a decent grip into the plastic; you can try, but you'll probably find the drill will slide away from our mark (and if you're unlucky into your hand). To beat this problem we'll start

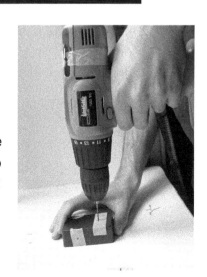

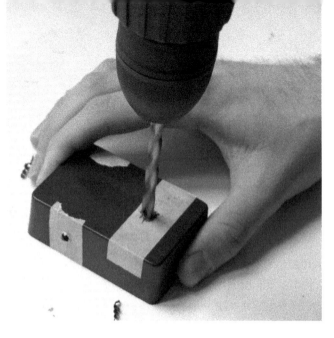

with a smaller drill size - try a 2mm bit, this thing will glide through plastic like anything.

After the 2mm, move onto a slightly larger size - 5mm. Finally drill the 6mm bit into the switch hole & the 8mm into the two input jack sockets.

Cool! Our pedal has now been drilled.

6. If you try and fit the parts through the holes now you'll probably find they won't fit. We need to file them down. The best technique for this is to keep moving in a circular motion with the file. Don't stay at one point to long or your carefully drilled circle will start to lose its shape! Stop every few rotations and see if the part fits (remember to hold the file at its handle as they can be sharp). Cool - we should now be able to screw in the parts to make sure everything fits. Does it look good? Great, that's the case finished. Unscrew and remove the part. It's now time to make the circuit!

Making The Circuit

Cut the Red Wire! (and the Black one)

The first thing I should point out is how dangerous a soldering iron can be: these things get hot, really hot! I'd recommend using a good quality stand while it's plugged in. Never touch the steel when it's turned on, only use the handle. Wait for it to cool down before putting it away - play it safe & leave it for at least 15 minutes before storing it again. If you treat it with respect you'll be ok! If you have any doubts find someone who can teach you the basics.

Ok, let's talk about the circuit: it's really very simple - when you press the switch, the current is broken & the audio cuts out. It's pretty much what happens in a light switch, except we're using it for audio! When you release the switch the circuit is restored and the audio returns again. Got that? Cool, let's set out and build the thing;

1. We're going to need some wire to connect the sockets and switch, let's start by cutting two equal amounts, about 10cm. I'll be using two colors, black & red, this is keep things simple but you can use just one color if that's all you have.

2. Now cut the red wire in half. You should now have three bits of wire (a long black one & two short red ones). We now need to strip the ends of plastic. You can use wire strippers or I find a Stanley knife works pretty well: strip about 7mm of plastic away from each of the ends of the wire. A good technique with the Stanley knife is to slice alongside the plastic away from you & then turn the wire, repeat, turn again & strip the remaining plastic:

Stripping Wire with a Box-Cutter

1. Place the box-cutter near horizontal along with the wire.

2. Start to slowly cut across.

3. Keep going slowly...

4. With a bit of luck the plastic should come away from the wire.

5. Now roll the wire to a different side and repeat.

3. Let's now hook-up the longer black wire: this wire's only going to connect from one jack socket to the other (we're saving the 'magic' for the two shorter red wires).

If you have the 'helping hands' tool, you can have it hold each input jack now, if not tape them down to keep them still.

Start by connecting the black wire to the **longer** jack socket solder connection points. To make sure it stays in place, hook and crimp with the pliers. Now the black wire should be able to hang all by itself.

Next we'll take the other end of black wire and hook it over the other longer solder point of the second jack.

Now before we move on any further just double check to make sure that you've connected the black wire the two longest connections (or rounded head to rounded head etc).

If your sockets have no identifiers you need to be careful here - if it's connected to differing sides the pedal will not work. That's not a big deal, you'll just have to re-solder it over to the correct side, but we'll try and do it correctly the first time, yes? Good!

We should now have something that looks like this:

Making Sure You've Attached the Wire to the Correct Point

Notice how one connector is slightly longer than the other? Also the tips are shaped differently to help distinguish it (one is flat, the other rounded).

Crimp My Style - An Example of Crimping

Make a hook in the wire using pliers.

Connect the hook. Notice how the end of the wire faces away from the other solder connection point. This will stop them from accidentally touching each other.

Now just squeeze the wire together with the pliers & we're finished crimping!

5. Now that we can be sure the black wire is going to the correct points we can now fire up the soldering iron; Place the soldering iron in its stand & turn it on. Only hold it by its handle from now on - it'll start heating up straight away but we'll need to leave it for a few minutes to make sure it's at a high enough temperature. If the stand came with a sponge, nows the time to go and wet it. If your stand came with no sponge use an old washing-up one. Wet it and rinse it of all the water - it should only be damp, not wet.

Universal Solder - Soldering the First Joint

Let's get busy and solder our first point. You've got some solder I hope? Cool.

Hold the soldering iron against the wire and connector, with your other hand push the solder into the tip of the soldering iron, wire & connector.

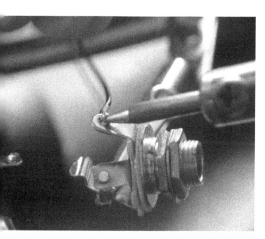

Keep pushing until it creates a small ball of solder around the tip of the wire & jack connector...

...keep pushing...

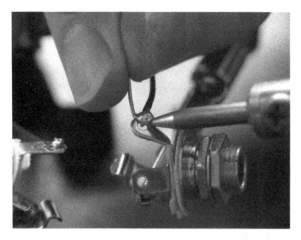

...a little bit more...

Lovely, that's our first solder joint completed.

Wipe away any excess solder on the sponge (this keeps our soldering iron happy).

6. Now solder the other end of the black wire to the remaining jack socket. All good? If you've messed up keep reading;

Fixing a Bad Solder Point

You've messed it up? I thought we weren't going to make any mistakes with this thing? Not to worry, it's easy to fix:

Fixing a bad point with a solder sucker

Heat the solder again, place the nib of the sucker next to it & suck it away from the joint. Repeat again if you need to.

Fixing a bad job with Solder flux

Heat the bad solder again until it becomes liquid, now place the flux into it, it should absorb the solder and then you're free to try again.

Fixing a bad point with no tools

Not recommended, but if you have no tool to deal with this you can always try reheating the solder and reshaping it with the soldering iron (maybe add some more solder too). Or try and remove the solder with the tip. Failing that, heat the solder and remove the wire completely - trim the wire and start again.

Attaching the Red Wire to the Foot Switch

If you've attached both ends the black wire to the jack sockets correctly then we've nearly completed our pedal! This is great, well done! Now let's finish with the red wire:

1. First let's connect one end of each of the red wires to the the remaining connections points of the jack sockets. Solder them as you did with the black wire. Awesome. Now we just need to connect the last red wire ends to the foot switch.

2. Connect one end of the red wire to one of the connection points on the foot switch. Now connect the other red wire to the remaining foot switch connection point. Don't worry about which side the foot switch is connected: it'll work either way, but let's make it look professional & have the left side of the switch connect to the left jack socket etc. Now we just need to solder these points and our circuit should be complete!

Soldering the Foot Switch

We'll solder exactly the same way as with the black wire.

Push the solder into the iron, connector and wire...

...until a small ball of solder begins to develop...

Nearly there...

Lovely. Wipe of any remaining solder, then finish the other side of the switch.

3.

Our circuit should now be complete! you should have something that looks like this;

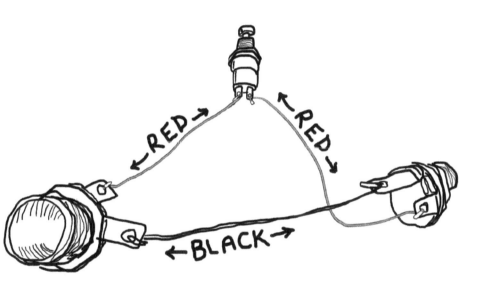

Well done; we just need to fix it into the case & we're ready to start rocking!

Attaching The Case To The Circuit

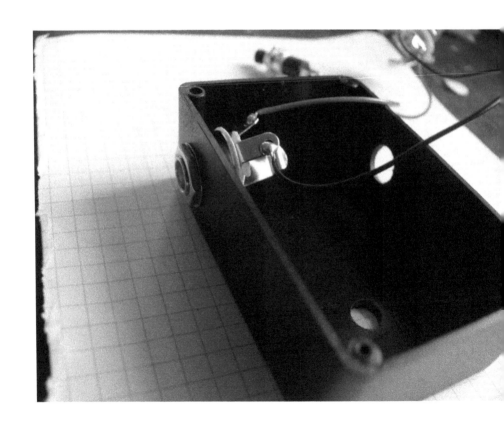

Let's Finish This!
Attaching the Circuit to the Case

Nows the time to remove the masking tape.

You should start by attaching the jack inputs to the case - hold onto the back of the socket as you tighten the bolt with the pliers, otherwise it may spin and disconnect our awesome soldering. The same is especially true with the foot switch, this sucker just wants to tear free but we're not going to let it, are we?

The foot switch that I'm using came with a round ring (ok scientist, a washer) but I've found without it I can make a more secure connection to the case.

Before we attach the back panel lets plug in a couple of guitar leads to make sure they don't touch each over. It's all good, no? If not, unscrew one of the sockets and use your file & head in a direction away from the other socket. Hopefully the washer of the jack socket will hide this little indiscretion!

When tightening the bolts make sure the parts don't twist around and snap the soldering!

Now all we need to do is attach the plastic feet on the case & then screw it together.
Congratulations: Your pedal is now finished!

Lets try this mother!

Plug your guitar jack in one side of the pedal (it doesn't matter which one) and then the other socket to your amp. Now strum without your foot on the pedal - you should hear your normal guitar (hopefully anyway if you've made it right!). Now strum again and press the pedal - it should cut the signal dead. Pretty cool, huh? No, ok, it's not the greatest pedal every but we've mad it together and that should mean something, right? I like to hold down the pedal, strum a note & release your foot. It's sort of like a poor mans volume pedal. Another cool effect is to quickly press the switch to make a stutter effect, or of course you can use it just to stop the signal.

F.A.Q

What to do if the Pedal Doesn't Work?

Don't Panic!

If something's gone wrong read on;

Incorrect Wiring:

If your new pedal isn't working, then my first guess would be that it's wired incorrectly. Go back & see if your circuit matches the diagram in this book. I betcha that's the problem! Re-solder into the correct positions & see if it doesn't work now.

Still not working? Read on...

Exposed wire is touching something?

Make sure no parts of the exposed wire (you know, the end of the wire that we stripped naked) isn't touching anything . If they are cover them with tape.

The Switch may be faulty or the wrong type:

I once was sent 'push to make' switches instead of 'push to break'! Can you imagine my face? Make sure you've ordered the correct type of switch. If it's the correct type then maybe it's possible you've been sent a dud?

Are the guitar jacks touching each other?

File down the case more to make them further apart.

Are you using the correct Wire?

Are you using 22 gauge solid copper wire? Are you sure?

Is the wire split or torn apart anywhere?

Is the solder point good enough? Has the solder fallen off???

Are you using a 1/4" Mono Jack Socket?

It May be a Fault in the Wire

Cut some new pieces of wire & replace the old ones.

Maybe you are Cursed?

Send me an email if you're really stuck: gary909@gmail.com

Thanks For Reading &

Enjoy Your Pedal!

Lightning Source UK Ltd.
Milton Keynes UK
UKHW021258291122
413061UK00021B/750